GRATITUDE JOURNAL

& DEVOTIONAL FOR KIDS

RAISING PURPOSEFUL, PRAYERFUL AND MINDFUL CHILDREN

By Jessica Lewis

Typesetting: Kerry Ellis

Cover Design: Olivier Darbonville

A CIP record for this book is available from the Library of Congress Cataloging-in-Publication Data

ISBN: 978-0-9834724-6-9

Printed by Corporate Color Printing Inc.

TIPS

TO GET THE MOST
OUT OF THIS JOURNAL:

1 Commit to completing it
regularly (preferably daily).

2 There is no wrong answer.

3 You may not understand some
of the Bible verses:

- Listen for God's understanding

- Ask an adult

- Write your best answer

4 Have fun!

My hope and intention is that this journal
radically transforms how you view Jesus,
the world, and yourself.

Date: March 22 - 2020

Name 3 foods you
are grateful for:

1. Pizza

2. ~~Banan~~ Banana's

3. Pesto Pasta

Verse of the Day

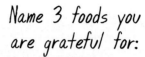 *Then God said, 'I give you every*

seedbearing plant on the face of

the whole earth and every tree that

has fruit with seed in it. They will

be yours for food.'

Genesis 1:29 NIV

What did you learn from the verse of the day?

how god BLeSSed us with food to eat, and how grateful we Should Be Because what if he didn't make food for us?

Prayer

Thank you Lord for creating the Earth and everything you have blessed it with. Help me to give thanks to you each time I eat.

My Prayer

God, I need help with...

my friends helpme make more when i go Back to school, and please help gramPa's foot heal fast.

Date: _____

Write 3 reasons why you
are grateful for your home:

1. _____

2. _____

3. _____

Verse of the Day

66 *Therefore, everyone who hears*

these words of mine and puts them

into practice is like a wise man who

built his house on the rock.

Matthew 7:24 NIV

Wise = knowing the right thing to do at the right time.

What did you learn from the verse of the day?

_____

_____

_____

Prayer

Lord, thank you for the place I live. Help me follow your commandments, love you with all my heart, and listen to the words of the adults that care for me.

My Prayer

Lord, show me how to...

_____

_____

_____

Date: March -23- 2020

Name 3 friends
you're grateful for:

1. Victoria

2. liegh

3. ava

Verse of the Day

66 *Treat others the same way you want*

them to treat you.

Luke 6:31 NASB

What did you learn from the verse of the day?

to treat others how i would like to be treated.

Prayer

Father in Heaven, thank you for my friends. Help me to treat them the way I would want to be treated.

My Prayer

God, help me be a better friend by...

Doing what they want to Do sometimes.

Date: _____

Write 3 reasons you are grateful for
your parents, grandparents or family:

1. _____

2. _____

3. _____

Verse of the Day

66 *Children, obey your parents in*

everything, for this pleases the

Lord.

Colossians 3:20 NIV

What did you learn from the verse of the day?

_____

_____

_____

Prayer

God, thank you for my parents. Help me listen
to them and do what is right in your sight.

My Prayer

God, help me listen to my parents better by...

_____

_____

_____

Date: march-24-2020

Name 3 things in nature
you are grateful for:

1. animals

2. waterfalls

3. ocean

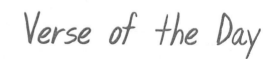

Verse of the Day

❝ *The earth and everything on it*

belong to the LORD. The world

and its people belong to Him. The

LORD placed it all on the oceans

and rivers.

Psalm 24:1-2 CEV

What did you learn from the verse of the day?

the world and everything on/in it Belong to God.

Prayer

God, thank you for all the things you have created. Help me take care of the earth as you would.

My Prayer

God, help me take better care of...

tests, let me DO good on them

Date: _____

Write 3 things about yourself
that you are grateful for:

1. _____

2. _____

3. _____

Verse of the Day

" Then God said, 'Let us make mankind in our image, in our likeness, so that they may rule over the fish in the sea and the birds in the sky, over the livestock and all the wild animals, and over all the creatures that move along the ground.' So God created mankind in own image, in the image of God, He created them; male and female He created them.

Genesis 1:26-27 NIV

What did you learn from the verse of the day?

_____

_____

_____

Prayer

Father in Heaven, thank you for creating me in your own image. Help me to see the special ways you made me different from everyone else.

My Prayer

God, I thank you for making me good at...

_____

_____

_____

Date: _____

Name 3 things about God you are grateful for:

1. _____

2. _____

3. _____

Verse of the Day

" *Our Lord and God, you are worthy*

to receive glory and honor and

power, because you have created

all things, and by your will they exist

and were created.

Revelations 4:11 CSB

Worthy = deserving
Glory = greatness deserving admiration
Honor = thought about highly

What did you learn from the verse of the day?

_____

_____

_____

Prayer

God, thank you for being patient, loving
and providing all my needs. Help me
grow closer to you every day.

My Prayer

God, help me grow closer to you by...

_____

_____

_____

Date: april 13,

Write 3 things about your teacher that you're grateful for:

1. She's smart.

2. She's kind to us.

3. She can always make lessons fun.

Verse of the Day

66 *For everything that was written in the past was written to teach us, so that through the endurance taught in the Scriptures and the encouragement they provide we might have hope.*

Romans 15:4 NIV

Endurance = power to finish something even when it seems difficult.

What did you learn from the verse of the day?

I learned scriptures
in the encouregment they
provide we may have hope.

Prayer

God, thank you for my teacher. Thank
you for the time, attention, and ways
they help me to learn new things.

My Prayer

God, help me to be a better student by...

giving mrs. maejakerzak
grade she works late
making fun lessons forus.

Date: _____

Write 3 things that happened yesterday that you're grateful for:

1. _____

2. _____

3. _____

Verse of the Day

66 *But if we confess our sins to God,*

He can always be trusted to forgive

us and take our sins away.

1 John 1:9 CEV

Confess = to admit or tell

What did you learn from the verse of the day?

_____

_____

_____

Prayer

God, thank you for forgiving me for the things I have done wrong and confessed to you. Help me to always ask for forgiveness when I do things the wrong way.

My Prayer

God, forgive me for…

_____

_____

_____

Date: _____

Name 3 sports or games
you are grateful for:

1. _____

2. _____

3. _____

Verse of the Day

66 *The city streets will be filled with*

boys and girls playing there.

Zechariah 8:5 NIV

What did you learn from the verse of the day?

_____

_____

_____

Prayer

God, I thank you for the fun I get to have.
Help me to act honestly and fair when I
play games and interact with people.

My Prayer

God, help me to be more honest about…

_____

_____

_____

Date: _____

Name 3 people you are grateful for:

1. _____

2. _____

3. _____

Verse of the Day

❝ *The righteous choose their friends*

carefully, but the way of the wicked

leads them astray.

Proverbs 12:26 NIV

Righteous = people who always do the right thing.
Wicked = sinful

What did you learn from the verse of the day?

_____

_____

_____

Prayer

God, thank you for my friends. Help me choose the right friends that you would want me to have.

My Prayer

God, the friends you would want me to have are...

_____

_____

_____

Date: _____

Name 3 places you
are grateful for:

1. _____

2. _____

3. _____

Verse of the Day

" " *I have told you these things, so that in me you may have peace. In this world you will have trouble. But take heart! I have overcome the world.*

John 16:33 NIV

Overcome = to successfully handle a problem

What did you learn from the verse of the day?

_____

_____

_____

Prayer

Father in heaven, thank you for giving me peace.
Help me to pray when I feel unsettled or uneasy.

My Prayer

God, I need your peace and want
to feel better about...

_____

_____

_____

Date: _____

Name 3 things in your room
that you are grateful for:

1. _____

2. _____

3. _____

Verse of the Day

" *If someone has enough money to*

live well and sees a brother or sister

in need but shows no compassion-

how can God's love be in that

person?

1 John 3:17 NLT

Compassion = care for what someone else is going
through.

What did you learn from the verse of the day?

_____

_____

_____

Prayer

God, thank you for my toys, clothes, and games.
Help me to help others that are in need.

My Prayer

God, a person I can help is...

_____

By...

_____

_____

Date: _____

Name 3 people in your
family you are grateful for:

1. _____

2. _____

3. _____

Verse of the Day

66 *The spirit himself testifies with our*

spirit that we are God's children.

Romans 8:16 NIV

Testify = to give proof.

What did you learn from
the verse of the day?

_____

_____

_____

Prayer

God, thank you for making me your
child. Help me to feel your love and
presence every day of my life.

My Prayer

God, help me to love others by...

_____

_____

_____

Date: _____

Write 3 reasons you are
grateful for your body:

1. _____

2. _____

3. _____

Verse of the Day

66 *Don't you realize that your body is
the temple of the Holy Spirit, who
lives in you and was given to you by
God? You do not belong to yourself,
for God bought you with a high
price. So you must honor God with
your body.*

1 Corinthians 6:19-20 NLT

Realize = to know/to understand

What did you learn from the verse of the day?

_____

_____

_____

Prayer

Thank you for creating my body the way
it is. Help me to see myself as you do.

My Prayer

God, help me to take better care of my body by...

_____

_____

_____

Date: _____

Name 3 people you love and are grateful for:

1. _____

2. _____

3. _____

Verse of the Day

" Then Christ will make his home in your hearts as you trust in Him. Your roots will grow down into God's love and keep you strong. And may you have the power to understand, as all God's people should, how wide, how long, how high, and how deep his love is.

Ephesians 3:17-18 NLT

What did you learn from the verse of the day?

_____

_____

_____

Prayer

Lord, thank you for your constant love. Help me
to pray and ask for your love when I need it.

My Prayer

Lord, help me act more loving and kind to...

_____

By...

_____

_____

Date: _____

Write 3 ways God made you
different from everyone else:

1. _____

2. _____

3. _____

Verse of the Day

" *You were saved by faith in God,*

who treats us much better than we

deserve. This is God's gift to you,

and not anything you have done

on your own. It isn't something you

have earned, so there is nothing

you can brag about.

Ephesians 2:8-9 CEV

What did you learn from the verse of the day?

_____

_____

_____

Prayer

God, thank you for creating me different than everyone else. Help me to see myself through your eyes; perfect, loved, special, unique, and gifted.

My Prayer

God, when I see people that are different than me I...

_____

_____

Help me to...

_____

Date: _____

Name 3 sweet things
you're grateful for:

1. _____

2. _____

3. _____

Verse of the Day

66 *Kind words are like a honeycomb,*

sweet to the soul and healing to

the bones.

Proverbs 16:24 NLT

What did you learn from the verse of the day?

_____

_____

_____

Prayer

God, thank you for words and the power they have. Help me to use kind words with others.

My Prayer

God, the person I want to be nicer to is....

_____

I will be nicer to them by...

_____

_____

Date: _____

Name 3 feelings you
are grateful for:

1. _____

2. _____

3. _____

Verse of the Day

" *Don't worry about anything; instead,*

pray about everything. Tell God

what you need, and thank Him for

all He has done.

Philippians 4:6 NLT

What did you learn from the verse of the day?

_____

_____

_____

Prayer

God, thank you for always being available for me to pray to. Lord, remind me to pray in all situations, even when I am happy, sad, worried, joyful or angry.

My Prayer

God, I worry about...

_____

_____

Help me to pray when I start to worry.

Date: _____

Write 3 of your
favorite Bible stories:

1. David and goliath

2. the story of Joseph

3. _____

Verse of the Day

" *You will seek me and find me when you search for me with all your heart.*

Jeremiah 29:13 ISV

What did you learn from the verse of the day?

_____

_____

_____

Prayer

God, thank you for the Bible and making yourself known to me through the stories that are in it. Help me to read your stories and understand more about you each time.

My Prayer

God, I only read the Bible when...

_____

_____

Help me read it...

Date: March 27

Name 3 things that are hot or
warm that you are grateful for:

1. warm Pizza

2. Mr. French

3. Sun

Verse of the Day

66 *If you forgive those who sin against*

you, your heavenly Father will

forgive you. But if you refuse to

forgive others, your Father will not

forgive your sins.

Matthew 6:14-15 NLT

What did you learn from the verse of the day?

it means to forgive others

Prayer

Father in heaven, thank you for sending your son Jesus to die on the cross and raising Him back to life, so that my sins may be forgiven. Help me to forgive others as you have forgiven me.

My Prayer

God, I forgive...

the Hacky sack

For... harting my Brother.

Date: _____

Write 3 reasons you
are grateful for water:

1. _____

2. _____

3. _____

Verse of the Day

" Then Moses raised his hand over the sea, and the Lord opened up a path through the water with a strong east wind. The wind blew all that night, turning the seabed into dry land. So the people of Israel walking through the middle of the sea on dry ground, with walls of water on each side!

Exodus 14:21-22 NLT

What did you learn from the verse of the day?

_____

_____

_____

Prayer

God, thank you for stories like this, stories
that show me how much you love your
people. Lord, help me to see your love
and compassion as I read the Bible.

My Prayer

God, I doubt you when...

_____

Give me greater belief in...

_____

_____

Date: _____

Write 3 reasons you are grateful for food:

1. _____

2. _____

3. _____

Verse of the Day

66 *Jesus answered, 'The Scriptures say: No one can live only on food. People need every word that God has spoken.'*

Matthew 4:4 CEV

What did you learn from the verse of the day?

_____

_____

_____

Prayer

God, thank you for your teachings in the Bible. Help me to see that your commandments are to keep me safe from all my challenges and temptations, and not to limit what I can do.

My Prayer

God, forgive me for...

_____

_____

_____

Date: _____

Write 3 reasons you are grateful
for your home or place you live:

1. _____

2. _____

3. _____

Verse of the Day

" You know that the Lord your God

is the only true God. So love Him

and obey his commands, and He

will faithfully keep his agreement

with you and your descendants for

a thousand generations.

Deuteronomy 7:9 CEV

The 10 Commandments:

1. Love God more than anything else
2. Don't make anything more important than God
3. Always say God's name with love and respect
4. Honor God by resting on the
   7th day of the week
5. Love and respect your mom and dad
6. Never murder anyone
7. Always be faithful to your husband or wife
8. Don't take anything that isn't yours
9. Always tell the truth
10. Be happy with what you have. Don't
    wish to have other people's things.

Prayer

God, thank you for showing me how to
live according to your commandments.

My Prayer

God, the commandments I need
the most help with are...

_____

_____

_____

Date: _____

Write 3 reasons you are
grateful for your school:

1. _____

2. _____

3. _____

Verse of the Day

" *Respect and obey the LORD! This is*

the beginning of knowledge. Only

a fool rejects wisdom and good

advice.

Proverbs 1:7 CEV

What did you learn from the verse of the day?

_____

_____

_____

Prayer

God, thank you for my school. Help me to
stay thankful for all I get to learn every day.

My Prayer

God, help me to be a better student by...

_____

_____

_____

Date: _____

Name 3 things in your house
that you are grateful for:

1. _____

2. _____

3. _____

Verse of the Day

" We know that all things work

together for the good of those

who love God- those whom He has

called according to his plan.

Romans 8:28 GW

What did you learn from the verse of the day?

_____

_____

_____

Prayer

God, thank you for working to make all things for my good. Help me to remember that you are in control always.

My Prayer

God, I worry about...

_____

_____

Help me to pray and trust that you will handle it all.

_____

Date: _____

Name 3 animals in the sea
you are grateful for:

1. _____

2. _____

3. _____

Verse of the Day

❝ *God said, 'I command the ocean to be full of living creatures, and I command birds to fly above the earth.' So God made the giant sea monsters and all the living creatures that swim in the ocean. He also made every kind of bird. God looked at what He had done, and it was good.*

Genesis 1:20-21 CEV

Command = to instruct or tell.

What did you learn from the verse of the day?

_____

_____

_____

Prayer

God, thank you for creating animals.
Help me to see your creativity and vast
imagination when I see animals.

My Prayer

God, help to be more creative by...

_____

_____

_____

Date: _____

Name 3 things that fly
that you are grateful for:

1. _____

2. _____

3. _____

Verse of the Day

" God blessed them; and said to them,

'Be fruitful and multiply, and fill the

earth, and subdue it; rule over the

fish of the sea and over the birds of

the sky and over every living thing

that moves on the earth.'

Genesis 1:28 NASB

Subdue = to suppress or to control

What did you learn from the verse of the day?

_____

_____

_____

Prayer

God, thank you for giving me the ability to care for the things that you have created. Show me ways I can care for your creation just as you would.

My Prayer

God, I want to take better care of...

_____

_____

_____

Date: _____

Name 3 things that grow
that you are grateful for:

1. _____

2. _____

3. _____

Verse of the Day

" *Jesus answered: Love the Lord your God with all your heart, soul and mind. This is the first and most important commandment. The second most important commandment is like this one. And it is, 'Love others as much as you love yourself.'*

Matthew 22:37-39 CEV

What did you learn from the verse of the day?

_____

_____

_____

Prayer

Lord, thank you for teaching me how to
live and treat others right. Help me to love
you above everything else in this world.

My Prayer

God, I love you because…

_____

_____

_____

Date: _____

Name 3 noises or sounds
that you are grateful for:

1. _____

2. _____

3. _____

Verse of the Day

66 *Every good present and every*

perfect gift comes from above,

from the Father who made the

sun, moon, and stars. The Fathers

doesn't change like the shifting

shadows produced by the sun and

the moon.

James 1:17 GW

What did you learn from the verse of the day?

_____

_____

_____

Prayer

God, thank you for allowing me to hear sounds. Help me to praise and worship you daily with my own voice.

My Prayer

God, help me this week with...

_____

_____

_____

CHECK IN POINT

GO BACK AND SEE:

What prayers has God answered?

_____

_____

_____

_____

What prayers do you need
to continue to pray?

_____

_____

_____

_____

How are you thinking different
since starting this journal?

_____

_____

_____

_____

How are you acting different
since starting this journal?

_____

_____

_____

_____

Date: _____

Write 3 reasons you're
grateful for today:

1. _____

2. _____

3. _____

Verse of the Day

❝ *'For I know the plans I have for you,'*

declares the Lord, 'plans to prosper

you and not to harm you, plans to

give you hope and a future. Then

you will call on me and come and

pray to me and I will listen to you.'

Jeremiah 29:11-12 NIV

What did you learn from the verse of the day?

_____

_____

_____

Prayer

Lord, thank you for the hope you have given me. Help me to pray when things are hard and when things are good.

My Prayer

Lord, I need you when...

_____

_____

_____

Date: _____

Name 3 things that smell good
that you are grateful for:

1. _____

2. _____

3. _____

Verse of the Day

66 *May the God of hope fill you with all*

joy and peace as you trust in Him,

so that you may overflow with hope

by the power of the Holy Spirit.

Romans 15:13 NIV

What did you learn from the verse of the day?

_____

_____

_____

Prayer

God, thank you for giving me the ability to smell and taste the amazing food you provide me with.

My Prayer

God, help me trust you with...

_____

_____

_____

Date: _____

Name 3 places you
are grateful for:

1. _____

2. _____

3. _____

Verse of the Day

66 *Give thanks to the Lord, proclaim*

his name; make known among the

nations what He has done. Sing to

Him, sing praise to Him; tell of all

his wonderful acts.

1 Chronicles 16:8-9 NIV

What did you learn from the verse of the day?

_____

_____

_____

Prayer

Lord, thank you for all the different cities and places you have created. Help me to think of you and give you all the glory and wonder as I am given opportunities to visit new places.

My Prayer

Lord, I normally praise you when...

_____

Help me to praise you...

_____

Date: _____

Write 3 things that you're grateful you can do:

1. _____

2. _____

3. _____

Verse of the Day

66 *But those who trust in the Lord*

will find new strength. They will be

strong like eagles soaring upward

on wings; they will walk and run

without getting tired.

Isaiah 40:31 CEV

What did you learn from the verse of the day?

_____

_____

_____

Prayer

Lord, thank you for the strength you have given me. Help me to see and know that all my strength, gifts, and talent come from you.

My Prayer

Lord, I need your strength with...

_____

_____

_____

Date: _____

Name 3 things you've done with your
family or friends that you're grateful for:

1. _____

2. _____

3. _____

Verse of the Day

66 *There is nothing better for a person*

than to eat, drink and enjoy his

work. I have seen that even this is

from God's hand, because who can

eat and who can enjoy life apart

from Him?

Ecclesiastes 2:24-25 CSB

What did you learn from the verse of the day?

_____

_____

_____

Prayer

Lord, I thank you for giving the ability to eat and drink with the people I love. Help me to appreciate the people around me even more.

My Prayer

Lord, I don't enjoy ...

_____

Help me to...

_____

_____

Date: _____

Name 3 things about God
that you are grateful for:

1. _____

2. _____

3. _____

Verse of the Day

❝ *I can do all things through Christ*

who strengthens me.

Philippians 4:13 NKJV

What did you learn from the verse of the day?

_____

_____

_____

Prayer

God, thank you for the forgiveness and patience that you have given me. Thank you for calling me your child and loving me like no one else can.

My Prayer

God, give me patience with...

_____

_____

_____

Date: _____

Name 3 movies you
are grateful for:

1. _____

2. _____

3. _____

Verse of the Day

" Give thanks to the Lord, for he is

good; his love endures forever.

Psalm 107:1 NIV

What did you learn from the verse of the day?

_____

_____

_____

Prayer

Lord, thank you for your unending love. Help me to love you above everything else.

My Prayer

Lord, help me spend more time with you by...

_____

_____

_____

Date: _____

Write 3 reasons why you
are grateful for your hands:

1. _____

2. _____

3. _____

Verse of the Day

" *Your right hand, O LORD, is glorious*

in power. Your right hand, O LORD,

smashes the enemy..

Exodus 15:6 NLT

What did you learn from the verse of the day?

_____

_____

_____

Prayer

God, thank you for creating me in your image.
Thank you for making me unique and special.

My Prayer

God, thank you for making me special by...

_____

_____

_____

Date: _____

Write 3 reasons why you
are grateful for your eyes:

1. _____

2. _____

3. _____

Verse of the Day

66 *You made all the delicate, inner parts*

of my body and knit me together in

my mother's womb. Thank you for

making me so wonderfully complex!

Your workmanship is marvelous-

how well I know it.

Psalm 139:13-14 NLT

What did you learn from
the verse of the day?

_____

_____

_____

Prayer

God, thank you for my ability to see. Help me
to see people and be kind to them as you do.

My Prayer

God, I will be kinder to...

_____

By...

_____

_____

Date: _____

Write 3 reasons why you are grateful
for the city or town you live in:

1. _____

2. _____

3. _____

Verse of the Day

" *O LORD, you have examined my heart and know everything about me. You know when I sit down or stand up. You know my thoughts even when I'm far away. You see me when I travel and when I rest at home. You know everything I do.*

Psalm 139:1-3 NLT

What did you learn from the verse of the day?

_____

_____

_____

Prayer

God, thank you for the place I live. Help me to fill it with things that are good and pleasing to you.

My Prayer

God, help me to stop...

_____

_____

_____

Date: _____

Write 3 things that happen during the morning that you are grateful for:

1. _____

2. _____

3. _____

Verse of the Day

" *Each morning let me learn more about your love because I trust you. I come to you in prayer, asking for your guidance. You are my God. Show me what you want me to do, and let you gentle Spirit lead me in the right path.*

Psalm 143:8,9 CEV

What did you learn from the verse of the day?

_____

_____

_____

Prayer

God, thank you for the good and bad things that happen in my life. Help me to trust that all things work out for good, for those who love you.

My Prayer

God, I don't understand why you allow...

_____

Help me...

_____

_____

Date: _____

Write 3 things that happen at
night that you are grateful for:

1. _____

2. _____

3. _____

Verse of the Day

66 *And God said, 'Let there be
light,' and there was light. God
saw that the light was good, and
he separated the light from the
darkness. God called the light 'day,'
and the darkness he called 'night'.
And there was evening, and there
was morning- the first day.*

Genesis 1:3-5 NIV

What did you learn from the verse of the day?

_____

_____

_____

Prayer

God, thank you for the stars in the sky. Help me to feel wrapped in your love, peace, and presence when I go to sleep tonight. Help me to feel secure by knowing you are looking over me.

My Prayer

God, I get scared of...

_____

Help me...

_____

_____

Date: _____

Write 3 reasons why you
are grateful for the Earth:

1. _____

2. _____

3. _____

Verse of the Day

" *In the beginning God created the heavens and the earth. The earth was barren, with no form of life; it was under a roaring ocean covered with darkness. But the Spirit of God was moving over the water.*

Genesis 1:1-2 CEV

What did you learn from the verse of the day?

_____

_____

_____

Prayer

God, thank you for the ocean and everything in it. Help me treat and care for the earth as you would want me to, with kindness and love.

My Prayer

God, I will take better care of the Earth by...

_____

_____

_____

Date: _____

Write 3 reasons why you
are grateful for winter time:

1. _____

2. _____

3. _____

Verse of the Day

" *Just as the heavens are higher than the earth, my thoughts and my ways are higher than yours. 'Rain and snow fall from the sky. But they don't return without watering the earth that produces seeds to plant and grain to eat. That's how it is with my words. They don't return to me without doing everything I send them to do.'*

Isaiah 55:9-11 CEV

What did you learn from the verse of the day?

_____

_____

_____

Prayer

God, thank you for the different seasons and temperatures. Help me to be reminded of your greatness when I see a flower blooming or a fallen leaf.

My Prayer

God, help me act differently when...

_____

_____

_____

Date: _____

Write 3 reasons why you
are grateful for summer time:

1. _____

2. _____

3. _____

Verse of the Day

" *Look at the birds. They don't plant or harvest or store food in barns, for your heavenly Father feeds them. And aren't you far more valuable to him than they are? Can all your worries add a single moment to your life?*

Matthew 6:26-27 NLT

What did you learn from the verse of the day?

_____

_____

_____

Prayer

Heavenly Father, thank you for the fun I have in the summertime. Help me to give all my worries to you. Fill me with your peace.

My Prayer

Heavenly Father, I worry about...

_____

When I begin to worry, help me...

_____

_____

Date: _____

Write 3 reasons why you
are grateful for your birthday:

1. _____

2. _____

3. _____

Verse of the Day

" *For we are God's masterpiece. He*

has created us anew in Christ Jesus,

so we can do the good things he

planned for us long ago.

Ephesians 2:10 NLT

What did you learn from the verse of the day?

_____

_____

_____

Prayer

Lord, thank you for my life. Help me to fully understand that I am your precious masterpiece.

My Prayer

Lord, help me to be the best person I can be by...

_____

_____

_____

Date: _____

Write 3 things that you are grateful
for that happened in the last week:

1. _____

2. _____

3. _____

Verse of the Day

" God showed his love for us when he
sent his only Son into the world to
give us life. Real love isn't our love
for God, but his love for us. God
sent his Son to be the sacrifice by
which our sins are forgiven. Dear
friends, since God loved us this
much, we must love each other.

1 John 4:9-11 CEV

What did you learn from the verse of the day?

_____

_____

_____

Prayer

God, thank you for sending your one and only son, Jesus, to die on the cross to forgive my sins. Help me forgive others as you have forgiven me.

My Prayer

God, I forgive...

_____

For...

_____

_____

Date: _____

Write 3 things that you have learned
in school that you are grateful for:

1. _____

2. _____

3. _____

Verse of the Day

" *Respect and obey the LORD! This is*

the beginning of knowledge. Only

a fool rejects wisdom and good

advice.

Proverbs 1:7 CEV

What did you learn from the verse of the day?

_____

_____

_____

Prayer

Lord, thank you for my brain and my ability to learn. Help me to stay humble and open to learning more about you.

Humble = not thinking you are better than anyone else.

My Prayer

Lord, I don't listen to...

_____

I will...

_____

_____

Date: _____

Write 3 things about your brain
that you are grateful for:

1. _____

2. _____

3. _____

Verse of the Day

" For the Lord grants wisdom! From his mouth come knowledge and understanding. He grants a treasure of common sense to the honest. He is a shield to those who walk with integrity. He guards the paths of the just and protects those who are faithful to Him.

Proverbs 2:6-8 NLT

What did you learn from the verse of the day?

_____

_____

_____

Prayer

Lord, thank you for protecting my path. Help me be honest and do what is right, even when no one is watching and even when it is hard.

My Prayer

Lord, I haven't been honest about...

_____

_____

_____

Date: _____

Name 3 things that are outside you are grateful for:

1. _____

2. _____

3. _____

Verse of the Day

" *In his hands are the depths of the earth; the heights of the mountains are his also. The sea is his, for He made it, and his hands formed the dry land.*

Psalm 95:4-5 ESV

What did you learn from the verse of the day?

_____

_____

_____

Prayer

Lord, thank you for all you have created, including me. Help me begin to understand all you have done and continue to do for me. Help me to realize that you are by my side every day.

My Prayer

God, I am most excited about...

_____

Help me...

_____

_____

Date: _____

Name 3 things that are round
that you are grateful for:

1. _____

2. _____

3. _____

Verse of the Day

66 *Don't be like the people of this*

world, but let God change the way

you think. Then you will know how

to do everything that is good and

pleasing to him.

Romans 12:2 CEV

What did you learn from the verse of the day?

_____

_____

_____

Prayer

God, thank you for my mind and my ability to learn. Help me to learn and follow the ways you want me to live.

My Prayer

God, I need help with...

_____

_____

_____

Date: _____

Name 3 parts of your body
that you are grateful for:

1. _____

2. _____

3. _____

Verse of the Day

" God has also given each of us
different gifts to use. If we can
prophesy, we should do it according
to the amount of faith we have.
If we can serve others, we should
serve. If we can teach, we should
teach. If we can encourage others,
we should encourage them. If we
can give, we should be generous.
If we are leaders, we should do our
best. If we are good to others, we
should do it cheerfully.

Romans 12:6-8 CEV

What did you learn from the verse of the day?

_____

_____

_____

Prayer

God, thank you for the things I am good at and the talent you have given me. Help me to use my gifts to serve you and others.

My Prayer

God, help me become better at...

_____

_____

_____

Date: _____

Write 3 reasons you
are grateful for food:

1. _____

2. _____

3. _____

Verse of the Day

66 *Jesus replied, 'I am the bread of life.*

Whoever comes to me will never

be hungry again. Whoever believes

in my will never be thirsty.'.

John 6:35 NLT

What did you learn from the verse of the day?

_____

_____

_____

Prayer

God, thank you for the food you have
provided. Help me to eat healthy
foods that are good for my body.

My Prayer

God, help me have better self-control with...

_____

_____

_____

Date: _____

What are 3 things that make you
laugh that you are grateful for:

1. _____

2. _____

3. _____

Verse of the Day

66 *We celebrated with laughter and*

joyful songs. In foreign nations, it

was said, 'The LORD has worked

miracles for his people.'

Psalm 126:2 CEV

What did you learn from the verse of the day?

_____

_____

_____

Prayer

God, thank you for my joy and happiness. Help me to find more joy in learning about you.

My Prayer

God, when I sing worship songs, help me to...

_____

_____

_____

Date: _____

What are 3 fun things
you are grateful for:

1. _____

2. _____

3. _____

Verse of the Day

" Whatever you do, do it from the

heart, as something done for the

Lord and not for people...

Colossians 3:23 CSB

What did you learn from the verse of the day?

_____

_____

_____

Prayer

God, thank you for the fun I have had. Help me to do all things for you, rather than the approval of my friends and what I want.

My Prayer

God, if someone talks bad about me I...

_____

_____

Help me know that, no matter what my friends think of me, you love me and your love is what matters.

Date: _____

Name 3 soft things that
you are grateful for:

1. _____

2. _____

3. _____

Verse of the Day

66 *Be kind to one another,*

tenderhearted, forgiving one

another, as God in Christ forgave

you.

Ephesians 4:32 ESV

What did you learn from the verse of the day?

_____

_____

_____

Prayer

God, thank you for all the people in my life. Help me to treat people just like you would treat them.

My Prayer

God, I will treat _____ better by...

_____

_____

Date: _____

Name 3 hard things
you are grateful for:

1. _____

2. _____

3. _____

Verse of the Day

" Consider it a great joy, my

brothers and sisters, whenever you

experience various trials, because

you know that the testing of your

faith produces endurance.

James 1:2-3 CSB

Endurance = ability to get through something tough.

What did you learn from the verse of the day?

_____

_____

_____

Prayer

God, thank you for the challenges I face in my life. Although challenges may not be easy to overcome, you promise to work them out for good for those who love you. Help me to be faithful and strong.

My Prayer

God, a challenge I need help with is...

_____

_____

_____

Date: _____

Name 3 things with wheels
that you are grateful for:

1. _____

2. _____

3. _____

Verse of the Day

" *No one undergoing a trial should*

say, 'I am being tempted by God,'

since God is not tempted by evil,

and He himself does not tempt

anyone.

James 1:13 CSB

Tempted = to have an urge or desire to do something
wrong.

What did you learn from the verse of the day?

_____

_____

_____

Prayer

God, thank you for not tempting me, instead making me strong. Help me and give me self-control when I want to do things I know I shouldn't.

My Prayer

God, I feel tempted by...

_____

Help me...

_____

_____

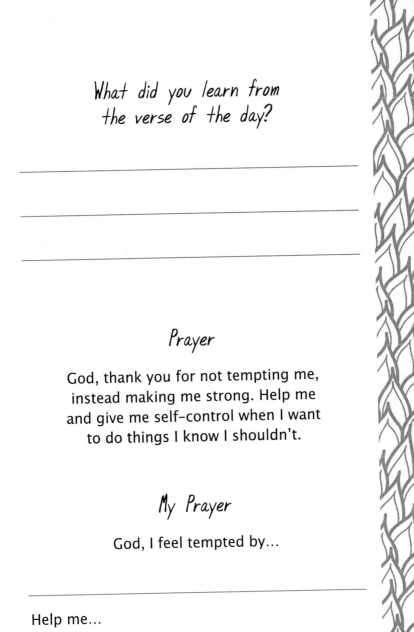

Date: _____

Name 3 green things that you are grateful for:

1. _____

2. _____

3. _____

Verse of the Day

" *Come to worship him with thankful hearts and songs of praise. The LORD is the greatest God, king over all other gods. He holds the deepest part of the earth in his hands, and the mountain peaks belong to him. The ocean is the Lord's because He made it, and with his own hands He formed the dry land.*

Psalm 95:2-5 CEV

What did you learn from the verse of the day?

_____

_____

_____

Prayer

Lord, thank you for giving me shelter. Help me to see the mountains, the sea, and the lands and be reminded that you created it all.

My Prayer

Lord, I have been ungrateful for...

_____

Help me to...

_____

_____

CHECK IN
POINT

LOOK BACK THROUGH
THE LAST 30 ENTRIES:

What prayers has God answered?

_____

_____

_____

What prayers do you need
to continue to pray?

_____

_____

_____

_____

Do you find yourself more
grateful throughout your day?
For what?

_____

_____

_____

_____

How is this journal changing
the way you think and act?

_____

_____

_____

_____

Date: _____

Name 3 red things
you are grateful for:

1. _____

2. _____

3. _____

Verse of the Day

66 *But as it is written,*

What no eye has seen, no ear has

heard, and no human heart has

conceived- God has prepared these

things for those who love him.

1 Corinthians 2:9 CSB

What did you learn from
the verse of the day?

_____

_____

_____

Prayer

God, thank you for all you have planned
for me. Help me to trust you and pray
in all good and difficult situations.

My Prayer

God, I don't understand why...

_____

_____

_____

Date: _____

What are 3 reasons you
are grateful to be alive:

1. _____

2. _____

3. _____

Verse of the Day

66 *Therefore, I tell you, whatever you*

ask for in prayer, believe that you

have received it, and it will be yours.

Mark 11:24

What did you learn from the verse of the day?

_____

_____

_____

Prayer

God, thank you for hearing all my prayers.
Help me to wait patiently when you choose not
to answer them the way I was hoping for.

My Prayer

God, a prayer you haven't answered yet is...

_____

Help me to...

_____

_____

Date: _____

Name 3 yummy foods
you are grateful for:

1. _____

2. _____

3. _____

Verse of the Day

" *Give to others, and God will give to you. Indeed, you will receive a full measure, a generous helping, poured into your hands- all that you can hold. The measure you use for others is the one that God will use for you.*

Luke 6:38 GNT

What did you learn from the verse of the day?

_____

_____

_____

Prayer

God, thank you for your fairness. You are the same yesterday, today, and forever. Help me to hear your lessons about being generous and become more generous like you.

My Prayer

God, I can be more generous by...

_____

_____

_____

Date: _____

Write 3 reasons you are grateful
to be a member of your family:

1. _____

2. _____

3. _____

Verse of the Day

" Peter then said: Now I am certain

that God treats all people alike.

God is pleased with everyone who

worships him and does right, no

matter what nation they come from.

Acts 10:34-35 CEV

What did you learn from
the verse of the day?

_____

_____

_____

Prayer

God, thank you for guiding me and helping me
to do the right thing. Please continue to help
me to make good decisions that please you.

My Prayer

God, help me...

_____

_____

_____

Date: _____

Write 3 reasons you are
grateful for a friend:

1. _____

2. _____

3. _____

Verse of the Day

66 *Jesus replied, 'All who love me*

will do what I say. My Father will

love them, and we will come and

make our home with each of them.

Anyone who doesn't love me will

not obey me.'

John 14:23-24 NLT

What did you learn from
the verse of the day?

_____

_____

_____

Prayer

Father in heaven, thank you for giving me the
exact ways to follow you; your commandments.
Give me self-control and strength to follow them.

My Prayer

Father in heaven, I need your help following
the commandment that says...

_____

_____

_____

Date: _____

What are 3 reasons you
are grateful for your nose:

1. _____

2. _____

3. _____

Verse of the Day

" Don't just pretend to love others.

Really love them. Hate what is

wrong. Hold tightly to what is good.

Romans 12:9 NLT

What did you learn from the verse of the day?

_____

_____

_____

Prayer

God, thank you for the love you give me.
I am so thankful to be your child. Help
me to love others as you would.

My Prayer

God, I will love my family better by...

_____

_____

_____

Date: _____

What are 3 reasons you are grateful
to be in the grade you are in:

1. _____

2. _____

3. _____

Verse of the Day

66 *Let you hope make you glad. Be*

patient in time of trouble and never

stop praying.

Romans 12:12 CEV

What did you learn from the verse of the day?

_____

_____

_____

Prayer

God, thank you for all I have to be happy about at school. Help me to be patient when things don't go the way I want them to. Help me to spread your joy at my school.

My Prayer

God, I need more patience with...

_____

_____

_____

Date: _____

Name 3 lunchtime foods
you are grateful for:

1. _____

2. _____

3. _____

Verse of the Day

" Everyone who calls on the name of

the Lord will be saved.

Romans 10:13 NIV

What did you learn from the verse of the day?

_____

_____

_____

Prayer

Lord, thank you for providing the healthy food that nourishes my body. Help me to be thankful for all that I have.

My Prayer

Lord, show me...

_____

_____

_____

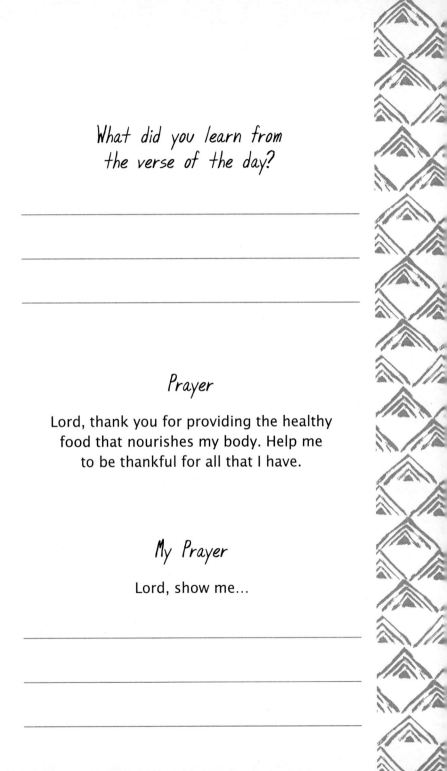

Date: _____

Name 3 dinnertime foods you are grateful for:

1. _____

2. _____

3. _____

Verse of the Day

❝ *And whatever you do, in word or in deed, do everything in the name of the Lord Jesus, giving thanks to the Father through him.*

Colossians 3:17 CSB

What did you learn from the verse of the day?

_____

_____

_____

Prayer

God, thank you for the time my family gets to spend together. Help me to do all things as if I am doing them for you.

My Prayer

God, I can do a better job at...

_____

_____

_____

Date: _____

Name 3 people you have helped
that you are grateful for:

1. _____

2. _____

3. _____

Verse of the Day

66 *Faith makes us sure of what we*

hope for and gives us proof of what

we cannot see.

Hebrews 11:1 CEV

What did you learn from the verse of the day?

_____

_____

_____

Prayer

God, thank you for the faith I have in you. Help me to deepen my belief and help me to rely on you more.

My Prayer

God, help me rely on you for...

_____

_____

_____

Date: _____

Name 3 reasons you are grateful for your legs:

1. _____

2. _____

3. _____

Verse of the Day

❝ *Love the Lord your God with all your heart and with all your soul and with all your strength.*

Deuteronomy 6:5 NIV

What did you learn from the verse of the day?

_____

_____

_____

Prayer

Lord, thank you for all the places my legs can take me to. Help me to appreciate and take care of my body, it is a gift from you.

My Prayer

Lord, I can show my love for you more by...

_____

_____

_____

Date: _____

What are 3 books you are grateful for:

1. _____

2. _____

3. _____

Verse of the Day

❝ *Love is patient and kind, never jealous, boastful, proud, or rude. Love isn't self-seeking, is not irritable, and does not keep a record of wrongs that others do.*

1 Corinthians 13:4-5 CEV

What did you learn from the verse of the day?

_____

_____

_____

Prayer

God, thank you for showing me how to love others. Help me to be patient, kind, and keep no records of wrongs for the people in my life.

My Prayer

God, forgive me for being impatient with...

_____

Help me to...

_____

_____

Date: _____

Write 3 things that make you
happy and you are grateful for:

1. _____

2. _____

3. _____

Verse of the Day

66 *Each person must make up your*

own mind about how much to give.

But don't feel sorry that you must

give and don't feel forced to give.

God loves people who love to give.

2 Corinthians 9:6-7 CEV

What did you learn from the verse of the day?

_____

_____

_____

Prayer

God, thank you for generously giving me
all that I have. Help me give to others, with
a joyful heart, when they are in need.

My Prayer

God, when I think about giving, the
person that comes to mind is...

_____

_____

I will...

_____

Date: _____

Name 3 ways you show
that you are grateful:

1. _____

2. _____

3. _____

Verse of the Day

66 *Kind words are good medicine, but*

deceitful words can really hurt.

Proverbs 15:4 CEV

What did you learn from the verse of the day?

_____

_____

_____

Prayer

Lord, thank you for telling me who I am, that I am dearly loved, forgiven, and set apart. Help me to say things to others that will build them up.

My Prayer

God, the person I will say something nice to is...

_____

I will tell them...

_____

_____

Date: _____

Write 3 reasons you are
grateful for your church:

1. _____

2. _____

3. _____

Verse of the Day

" *Don't get tired of helping others.*

You will be rewarded when the time

is right, if you don't give up. We

should help people whenever we

can, especially if they are followers

of the Lord.

Galatians 6:9-10 CEV

What did you learn from
the verse of the day?

_____

_____

_____

Prayer

God, thank you for helping me do things
that will help others. Help me to see the
needs of others and guide me to offer
help to them, just like you would.

My Prayer

God, I will help...

_____

_____

_____

Date: _____

What are 3 qualities about yourself
that you are grateful God gave you:

1. _____

2. _____

3. _____

Verse of the Day

66 *Some people trust in the power of*

chariots and horses, but we trust

you, LORD God.

Psalm 20:7 CEV

What did you learn from the verse of the day?

_____

_____

_____

Prayer

Lord, thank you for the ways you have made me special. Help me to remember that the things I am good at are gifts from you. Help me to use the gifts you have blessed me with to bless others.

My Prayer

God, one of the things I love about you is...

_____

_____

_____

Date: _____

What are 3 things you love
that you are grateful for:

1. _____

2. _____

3. _____

Verse of the Day

66 *Do your own work well, and then*

you will have something to be proud

of. But don't compare yourself with

others.

Galatians 6:4 CEV

What did you learn from the verse of the day?

_____

_____

_____

Prayer

God, thank you for the people I love
dearly in my life. Help me focus on you
so I can get my approval from you, while
not comparing myself to others.

My Prayer

God, I compare myself to...

_____

Help me to...

_____

_____

Date: _____

Name 3 furry or fuzzy
things you are grateful for:

1. _____

2. _____

3. _____

Verse of the Day

❝ *Obey the LORD and serve him*

faithfully with all your heart.

Remember the great things He has

done for you.

1 Samuel 12:24 GNT

What did you learn from the verse of the day?

_____

_____

_____

Prayer

Lord, thank you for all the great things you
have done for me in my life. Help me to
fully understand that all good and perfect
things are gifts that come from you.

My Prayer

Lord, I need your help to understand why...

_____

_____

_____

Date: _____

Name 3 Bible stories
that you are grateful for:

1. _____

2. _____

3. _____

Verse of the Day

66 *All Scripture is inspired by God and*

is useful to teach us what is true and

to make us realize what is wrong

in our lives. It corrects us when we

are wrong and teaches us to do

what is right.

2 Timothy 3:16 NLT

What did you learn from
the verse of the day?

_____

_____

_____

Prayer

God, thank you for giving me the Bible
as a guide. Help me to correct the
things that are wrong in my life.

My Prayer

God, forgive me for...

_____

_____

_____

Date: _____

What are 3 ways being
grateful makes you feel:

1. _____

2. _____

3. _____

Verse of the Day

66 *God's Spirit makes us sure that we*

are God's children.

Romans 8:16 CEV

What did you learn from the verse of the day?

_____

_____

_____

Prayer

God, thank you for giving me the
Holy Spirit. Help me to set aside quiet
time to listen to your guidance.

My Prayer

God, you tell me that I am...

_____

_____

_____

Date: _____

Write 3 experiences
you are grateful for:

1. _____

2. _____

3. _____

Verse of the Day

" 'Go out and stand before me on the mountain,' the LORD told him. And as Elijah stood there, the LORD passed by, and a mighty windstorm hit the mountain. It was such a terrible blast that the rocks were torn loose, but the LORD was not in the wind. After the wind there was an earthquake, but the LORD was not in the earthquake. And after the earthquake there was a fire, but the LORD was not in the fire. And after the fire there was a sound of a gentle whisper.

1 Kings 19:11-12 NLT

What did you learn from the verse of the day?

_____

_____

_____

Prayer

Lord, thank you for stories like this, stories that show me your great power. Help me to set time aside time to listen for your gentle whispers.

My Prayer

Lord, I can make time to listen to your voice by...

_____

_____

_____

Date: _____

What are 3 things found in the
sky that you are grateful for:

1. _____

2. _____

3. _____

Verse of the Day

" You fathers- if your children ask for
a fish, do you give them a snake
instead? Or if He asks for an egg,
do you give them a scorpion? Of
course not! If you then, who are
evil, know how to give good gifts
to your children, how much more
will your heavenly Father give the
Holy Spirit to those who ask him!

Luke 11:11-13 ESV

What did you learn from the verse of the day?

_____

_____

_____

Prayer

God, thank you for the gift of the Holy Spirit. Help me turn to you in prayer when I am frustrated, sad, stressed, happy, and joyful. In my good times and bad.

My Prayer

God, a hard situation where I need your help is...

_____

_____

_____

Date: _____

Name 3 people you saw last
week that you are grateful for:

1. _____

2. _____

3. _____

Verse of the Day

" *Then the Lord God formed a man of*

dust from the ground, and breathed

into his nostrils the breath of life;

and man, became a living being.

Genesis 2:7 NASB

What did you learn from the verse of the day?

_____

_____

_____

Prayer

Lord, thank you for my family and friends.
Help me to remember that everything good
comes from you, including the people I love.

My Prayer

God, help me to...

_____

_____

_____

Date: _____

What are 3 things you listen
to that you are grateful for:

1. _____

2. _____

3. _____

Verse of the Day

" *Finally, my friends, keep your minds*

on whatever is true, pure, right,

holy, friendly, and proper. Don't

ever stop thinking about what is

truly worthwhile and worthy of

praise.

Philippians 4:8 CEV

What did you learn from the verse of the day?

_____

_____

_____

Prayer

God, thank you for giving us ears to hear and a mind to think. Help me think about and listen to things that are pleasing to you.

My Prayer

God, help me re-focus my thoughts on your goodness when I start thinking about...

_____

_____

_____

Date: _____

Name 3 things that happened
yesterday that you are grateful for:

1. _____

2. _____

3. _____

Verse of the Day

66 *But I am like an olive tree growing*

in God's house, and I can count on

his love forever and ever.

Psalm 52:8 CEV

What did you learn from the verse of the day?

_____

_____

_____

Prayer

God, thank you that your love lasts forever and ever. Help me to be a light for you, so that your love can change the way I treat others.

My Prayer

God, help me to love...

_____

By...

_____

_____

Date: _____

What are 3 holidays
that you are grateful for:

1. _____

2. _____

3. _____

Verse of the Day

" *Examine me, O God, and know*

my mind. Test me, and know my

thoughts. See whether I am on

an evil path. Then lead me on the

everlasting path.

Psalm 139:23-24 GW

What did you learn from the verse of the day?

_____

_____

_____

Prayer

God, thank you for the fun I have had during the holidays. Help me to keep everything in my life in order. Above all, help me to keep you first.

My Prayer

God, something I do and know
that I shouldn't is...

_____

_____

Help me...

_____

Date: _____

Write 3 reasons you
are grateful for school:

1. _____

2. _____

3. _____

Verse of the Day

" *But his answer was: 'My grace is all you need, for my power is greatest when you are weak.' I am most happy, then, to be proud of my weaknesses, in order to feel the protection of Christ's power over me.*

2 Corinthians 12:9 GNT

What did you learn from the verse of the day?

_____

_____

_____

Prayer

God, thank you for helping me when I am weak.
Help me to pray without ceasing and spend time
with you when I feel discouraged and weak.

My Prayer

God, I feel weak when...

_____

Help me to...

_____

_____

Date: _____

Write 3 things you do when you're not
in school that you're grateful for:

1. _____

2. _____

3. _____

Verse of the Day

66 *He who conceals his sins doesn't*

prosper, but whoever confesses

and renounces them find mercy.

Proverbs 28:13 WEB

Renounce = to stop doing

What did you learn from the verse of the day?

_____

_____

_____

Prayer

God, thank you for forgiving me of all my sins. Help me to confess my sins and follow your ways each time I make a mistake.

My Prayer

God, a sin I need to confess is...

_____

_____

_____

Date: _____

Name 3 warm things
you are grateful for:

1. _____

2. _____

3. _____

Verse of the Day

66 *But the Lord said to Samuel, 'Don't*

judge by his appearance or height,

for I have rejected him. The LORD

doesn't see things the way you see

them. People judge by outward

appearance, but the LORD looks

at the heart.'

1 Samuel 16:7 NLT

What did you learn from the verse of the day?

_____

_____

_____

Prayer

Lord, help me not to like or dislike others because of how they seem on the outside. Help me see others by their character, just as you do.

My Prayer

God, I have judged or said mean things about...

_____

Help me to...

_____

_____

Date: _____

Name 3 things that make you
cold that you are grateful for:

1. _____

2. _____

3. _____

Verse of the Day

" *With the tongue we bless our Lord*

and Father, and with it we curse

people who are made in God's

likeness. Blessing and cursing come

out of the same mouth. My brothers

and sisters, these things should not

be this way.

James 3:9-10 CSB

What did you learn from the verse of the day?

_____

_____

_____

Prayer

Lord, thank you for giving me verses like this, it tells me exactly how to act and react. Help me to speak only good things to others.

My Prayer

Lord, help me see the goodness in...

_____

_____

_____

Date: _____

Write 3 reasons you
are grateful today:

1. _____

2. _____

3. _____

Verse of the Day

" God's spirit makes us loving, happy,

peaceful, patient, kind, good,

faithful, gentle, and self-controlled.

There is no law against behaving in

any of these ways.

Galatians 5:22 CEV

What did you learn from the verse of the day?

_____

_____

_____

Prayer

Thank you for all the blessings that come from your Spirit. Help me grow in the areas I am not good at.

My Prayer

God, I pray that your Spirit gives me more...

_____

_____

_____

CONGRATULATIONS!!!!!

YOU MADE IT THROUGH 90 ENTRIES OF GRATITUDE AND DEVOTIONALS.

I hope God moved in mighty ways
while you were completing your journal.

I pray that you can now see God
for who He is, others through His eyes
and yourself as the marvelous creation
He made you to be.

DON'T STOP HERE.

Visit
www.KidsGratitudeJournals.com
for our newest edition!

EMAIL
support@KidsGratitudeJournals.com
for the latest
DISCOUNT CODE!